HAL•LEONARD INSTRUMENTAL PLAY-ALONG

AUDIO ACCESS INCLUDED

PLAYBACK+
Speed • Pitch • Balance • Loop

SUPERHERO THEMES

Audio arrangements by Peter Deneff

To access audio, visit:
www.halleonard.com/mylibrary
Enter Code
2394-8972-9314-1220

ISBN 978-1-70513-163-3

Visit Hal Leonard Online at
www.halleonard.com

Contact us:
Hal Leonard
7777 West Bluemound Road
Milwaukee, WI 53213
Email: info@halleonard.com

In Europe, contact:
Hal Leonard Europe Limited
42 Wigmore Street
Marylebone, London, W1U 2RN
Email: info@halleonardeurope.com

In Australia, contact:
Hal Leonard Australia Pty. Ltd.
4 Lentara Court
Cheltenham, Victoria, 3192 Australia
Email: info@halleonard.com.au

THEME FROM ANT-MAN
from MARVEL'S ANT-MAN

HORN

Music by CHRISTOPHE BECK

WAKANDA
from BLACK PANTHER

Music by LUDWIG GÖRANSSON

THE AVENGERS
from THE AVENGERS

HORN

Composed by
ALAN SILVESTRI

BATMAN THEME

HORN

Words and Music by
NEAL HEFTI

CAPTAIN AMERICA MARCH
from CAPTAIN AMERICA

HORN

By ALAN SILVESTRI

ELASTIGIRL IS BACK

from INCREDIBLES 2

Horn

Composed by
MICHAEL GIACCHINO

IMMORTALS
from BIG HERO 6

Horn

Words and Music by ANDREW HURLEY,
JOE TROHMAN, PATRICK STUMP
and PETE WENTZ

Moderately
Synth

Play

mf

f

GUARDIANS INFERNO

from GUARDIANS OF THE GALAXY VOL. 2

HORN

Words and Music by JAMES GUNN
and TYLER BATES

9

THE INCREDITS

from THE INCREDIBLES

Horn

Music by MICHAEL GIACCHINO

POW! POW! POW! - MR. INCREDIBLES THEME

from INCREDIBLES 2

Horn

Music and Lyrics by
MICHAEL GIACCHINO

IRON MAN
from IRON MAN

HORN

By RAMIN DJAWADI

13

ROCKETEER END TITLES

from THE ROCKETEER

Horn

By JAMES HORNER

THEME FROM SPIDER MAN

HORN

Written by BOB HARRIS
and PAUL FRANCIS WEBSTER

X-MEN: APOCALYPSE - END TITLES
from X-MEN: APOCALYPSE

Horn

By JOHN OTTMAN